Schopenhauer - glory
Poe?
Céline}
Beddoes
not pessimistic, but

DOSTOYEVSKY
AND OTHER POEMS

or throwback to a time when it still made sense
to speak, as TM does in the epigraph to
of genius of disease, disease of genius

- Mystic horror (p.28) in

the political poems are the sort you'd expect a Cd
Ambassador to write. Cf° Wallace Stevens on anarchists

The literary — the voices
The sources he spoke about in an interview

Opinionated poems less good e.g. Taking Cover p.20

One c̄ Rozanov, Mann, [illegible] aide,, Nabokov
Why a dialogue c̄ Dosto.

DOSTOYEVSKY

AND OTHER POEMS

BY

personal
lonely

he seer s.t.
he remembers s.t.
it doesn't
care

Ohme on writing
It creates a dichotomy | diff in degree
well that depends

R.A.D. FORD

haunted
not haunting

self - possessed —

cf° Dosto.
intrigued by himself

Drawings and Illustrations

by

Ernst Neizvestny

MOSAIC PRESS

Oakville - New York - London

CANADIAN CATALOGUING IN PUBLICATION DATA

Ford, R.A.D., 1915-
Dostoyevsky and other poems

ISBN 0-88962-411-9

I. Title.

PS8511.072D68 1988   C811'.54   C88-094811-6
PR9199.3.F66D68 1988

Published by *MOSAIC PRESS*, P.O. Box 1032, Oakville, Ontario.
L6J 5E9, Canada. Offices and warehouse at 1252, Speers Road,
Unit #1 2, Oakville Ontario. L6L 5N9, Canada.

Published with the assistance of the Canada Council and the
Ontario Arts Council.

Drawings and Illustrations © Ernst Neizvestny, 1984. Repro-
duced by permission of Mosaic Press from *Ernst Neizvestny: Life
and Work*, published in 1984.
Cover Portrait Mask of Dostoyevsky by Ernst Neizvestny.
Copyright © R.A.D. FORD, 1988.
Design by Rita Vogel
Typeset by Aztext Electronic Publishing Ltd.
Printed and bound in Canada.

ISBN 0-88962-409-7 PAPER

In Canada:
        MOSAIC PRESS,1252 Speers Road Units# 1&2, Oakville,
Ontario L6L 5N9, Canada. P.O. Box 1032 Oakville, Ontario
Canada L6J 5E9

In the United States:
        Riverrun Press Inc., 1170 Broadway, Suite 807, New York,
N.Y., 10001, U.S.A., distributed by Kampmann & Co., 9 East 40th
Street, New York, N.Y., 10016

In the U.K.:
        John Calder (Publishers) Ltd., 18 Brewer Street, London,
W1R 4A5, England.

To

All the Poets
of Russia

Past
and
Present

PREVIOUS BOOKS OF POETRY by R.A.D. Ford

A Window on the North - 1956

The Solitary City - 1969

Holes in Space - 1979

Needle in the Eye - 1983

Russian Poetry - 1984

Doors, Words and Silence - 1985

Table of Contents

PART III - *The Window*

PART IV - *The Wound and the Bow*

PART V - The Shortest Poem

PART VI - Pozzi

I - *The Kingdom of Commagene*

The Kingdom of Commagene

The simplest of houses speaks to me of you,
The plainest of walls growing in stature,
But crumbling also and accumulating
Dark stains that every year seem
To spread wider after the latest fall of snow.

They have the shape and contours
Of ancient maps; one in particular
Singularly like the Terra de Labrador.
Another, without geography,
Becomes for me the tiny Kingdom
Of Commagene about which we know
Absolutely nothing.

Just a foot-note in the History
Of Cappadocia which is slight
Evidence that it ever existed.
Still the name suffices for me.

But take that little house, that cabin
Again. It changes before my eyes.
It has the sagging skin of an old man.
It too will disappear without honour,
And, having no stone or marble, will return
Its logs and plastered walls slowly
Into our northern jungle of pine and tamarack.

Leaving no more trace for another
Century than Commagene
And its Kingdom and a name
That will not let it die.

A Temporary Destination

Having walked all morning
Through the February woods
We have become the sound almost
Of footsteps. Between the smoke
Of mist frozen on the twigs
And trunks of trees we can
Distinguish our destination.

There is none really, but the heart
Makes it necessary to pretend:
Provisionally at least the lake,
White at mid-day with a sun
Bloody through the winter fog.

You tell me to speak lower.
At this time of year the woods
Are all ears, a presence more
Obvious every day, more intent
On listening to almost any
Conversation, no matter how
Totally banal.

      Returning from afar,
The land, the lake, while ours,
Seem alien. They appear to be
The very limits of being, perhaps
Added as an after-thought
By a distraught geographer
To an ancient map.

Inside the decrepit cabin on
The shore, once an idyll, a fantasy
When very young, first orphaned,
There is a hearth and soon
A fire. Enough to induce
Small white cries of joy.

And later with the smokey warmth
The alienation melts, and
Sleep, that subtle foe, moulds
Memories into stone.
Which are left stone beside
The lake seemingly smaller now.

Before night obscures the path
We go reluctantly back
The way we came.
Leaving our monuments behind
To gather moss and hide
Our unimportant history.

Voyageur Ami

"O voyageur ami, pere du souvenir".
Alfred de Musset

I feel a cold breeze
Out of the distant sky
Across the northern plain
Where almost imperceptibly
The prairie fades away
Into the futile scrub.

And your hand reaches mine
Beyond the years
Far traveller my adventurer
Spurning the wild water
Unafraid unperturbed
Wondering only.

And your mystic touch
As I reach the verge
Of your wilderness
Tells me my other friend
The voyager in the night
Is just a step behind
And paces me through the maze.

Ernst Neizvestny, Etchings from "Crime and Punishment".

An Organized World

My world, which revolves around
Small objects and I think well organized,
Slips gradually every day
Towards chaos. It is not
Unpleasant, being in the order of things,
And order being the overwhelming
Aim of man. But some disorder
Rationally sought might produce
The proper counterpoint — some useless
Exercise, some sleepy time spent
Dreaming of a universe not mine.
It might even briefly stop
The slide into oblivion.

Palmyra

Present decay, how can it be new?
It is submerged in the sleep
Of ages. The pines are dead
Or dying, the plane trees
Equally menaced and the Arctic fox
Leads a life of numbered days.

The fox means nothing to me.
I never saw one, white wraith
On the snow. But I care,
And my neighbour cares, cursing
If the lights go out or the gas
Flickers and is dead.

He screams on the telephone.
He rants at his wife and at me
Or what he thinks is me.
For I have gone secretly
Underground to commune
With Palmyra and her queen.

> "But I have the imagination of disaster
> and see life as ferocious and sinister"
> Henry James 1896

In a place with an improbable name
The fever of the city is close
To hate. You enter a small cafe.
It is full. They all seem friends
But their backs are turned away.
This is how every day ends.

There is no cause for alarm.
But since you live with the imagination
Of disaster the silence and the absence
Of faces excludes you from the touch
Of others.

      And you wonder
If it will be the same always
Even in cities whose names
Are familiar and pronounceable.

Taking Cover

There are times when it seems
Impossible to ignore the flotsam
That imposes itself, even if
One can selectively pick
Some true object from
The dump heap or detect
A pure melody from the waves
Of junk that assault our ears.

I can take cover, my hands,
My eyes can take cover,
Blocking out the overwhelming,
Miniscule and ever present
Refuse of our age.

       But some
Ancient usage tears my hands
From my eyes, destroys
What cover I thought to find
In blotting out the detritus
Of our time.

       Blindness
Is no solution for distaste.

Release

I have a part in this place
I have a small allotment of peace

I have assembled some silence
I have sold my share

Of reality and thrown away
The lawyers and notaries and their

Claim on my hoarded gold
And its guardian violence

And usuary government bonds
My pension mutual funds

I have no pin-prick of conscience
But joyfully am aware

I can now look at the sky
Without a backward glance

Or shiver of remorse
For time spent frivolously

And though I've no recourse
I think it all makes sense.

My Inheritance

Struggling most of my life it seems
Through the drifts of documents,
Notes and codicils, all now
Carefully fed into impossible
Computers that cannot lie but are
Invariably wrong, the real papers
Shredded in some
Obscene backroom,

      I suddenly
Realize they are all in error.
All I need to survive is love,
And a vast indifference
To coded telegrams announcing
Death and promising nothing.

Mondrian

White on white, perhaps black on black.
Defiance of the time has disappeared.
The first thrill of understanding half
A century ago has given way
To doubt. Is it really the perfection
Of nothing? Or is it nothing?

I am growing blind or old or both.
I can no longer distinguish between
Birch, beech or even hickory. Then
How or when do the leaves decide to go?
Some hold on like old men not
Wanting to give up. And I can
Feel for each leaf falling.

And I want to Know what white
On white first meant and if today
It has no more relevance than
Bouguereau in his prime.

And if it is no more than a blank
Page, then I prefer "plutot le chagrin
Que le neant".

My Own Republic

In the betraying days
Of early March I am

Looking with passion
For some-one to talk to.

Though I have nothing
New to say I hope

Haphazard conversation
Will let me learn

How to live without
Reproach, remorse

These untrustworthy
Days in this small

And nameless land
With its unknown tongue.

Which I probably
Merit having come

Perversely to it by
A way not recommended

By my betters or my peers.
Still March will soon have ended

And if Spring is here
I can put off looking

And be content to share
With no-one else

My private country
For another year.

Putting It Together

One solution
Seemed to be
To piece together
The fragments of time
The foolish moments
Passed without thinking
In a history
Without thought,

While collecting
Bits of lost space
Into an effort
At new world
Architecture.

     Yet
It appeared possible
Probable even
That the inevitable
Earthquake
Starting in Tierra
Del Fuego and moving
Surreptitiously north
Would make it all
Sadly laughable,

Not what started to be
The assembling
Into some new whole
Of a fragmented being.

Blind Night

I am afraid of these
Crippled days that stumble
Into the short nights of winter.

     They seem to lead
Clumsily into blank walls,
Smooth and cold to the touch,
Encompassing strange fields
Studded with rocks, and gray
With sodden snow.

I find no gates, and my hands
Transmit fear. I feel eyes
Following me from the wall,
Staring at me even in the winter dusk.

     All my walls
Have eyes. They keep me out,
Not in. All my fears are summed
Up in these seeing walls.
All my days are short and all
My nights blind.

The Augean Stables

Who else would come
And clean our stables
Of the filth accumulated
Through the months and years
But an innocent hand,
Unaccustomed, unready
For the Greeks, their legends
And the toil ahead.

The horses are gone all,
Long ago, and their victories.
I hardly remember them, their
Silken manes and golden hooves.
We live with the emptiness
Of deceits which smell.
Not lies but small
Deceptions and half truths.

In this age can I find
That hand? Will the stables be
Cleaned in time? Before death
Crooks his finger and slyly
Grins at me? Is it too much to ask?
A little help with my old-fashioned
Broom, a few hours more
In this numbing month of March.

Mystic Terror

I have no recollection now
Of words used cruelly

Uselessly perhaps but without
The intention to offend

Did I elaborate a perfect phrase
For an unnecessary wound?

Memory is too obscure
The will to forget too great

Words must follow
Into the other world

They are probably all
That will survive

In the mystic terror
That envelops us

Ernst Neizvestny, "Hermaphrodite". Drawing. Indian ink and color.

Balance

Umbram Fugat Veritas

Searching my life for
Equilibrium, which is truth,
I return to the Roman source.
Seeking to eliminate
The unessential, I find
My Latin roots again.
These words so precious, rare,
Occult. Spare, they say
Everything without a hint
Of decoration, untouched
By the erosion of time.

"Shadows flee truth."
English says it too, and I
Repeat them both, savouring
The economy of sound
For the maximum of sense.
It is a prescription against
The hyperbole of our age.

II - *A Dostoyevsky Cycle*

"I am filled with awe, with a profound mystic, silence-enjoining awe, in the presence of the religious greatness of the damned, in the presence of genius of disease and the disease of genius, of the type of the afflicted and the possessed, in whom saint and criminal are one."

— Thomas Mann on Dostoyevsky

Homage to Fyodor Mihailovich

"Na Nevsky bashne tishina"

("On the Nevsky bastion silence falls")
— Old Russian ballad

They are all with us still,
Eccentric, improbable and yet
More real than our familiars,
As solid as the Nevsky Gate.

All the madmen of time,
All the holy fools of God,
Assemble then to celebrate
Unwillingly their sad end.

They walk like robots through
His city in the untender dawn,
Bearing no message visible,
But understood by all.

And we reach you through the years
To touch your wondering soul,
And are stronger for the word
And brave for what we heard.

The Disease of Genius

He has a legalised
Complaint to make

Against the landscape
Of his fate,

Against the cold
And obdurate rain

That since his childhood
Moulded him.

And turned each rare
And sparkling day

Into a travesty
Of peace.

Let him walk silently
To his small place,

Buried in the ever
Devious slums.

There finally to forget
The falling sickness fever,

Taking the few crumbs
Of love that fell

From the tables of the poor
And alone remember

The winter weather

of his special Hell.

Prince Myshkin

I have a holy fool inside.
He weighs each word I say.
And when I talk coherently
I feel him drift away,

Walk into the midnight fog,
And wrap himself around
A derelict, a pimp, a fag
For company underground.

Or make a holy sacrifice,
Idle in the streets once more,
Wearing an uncertain face,
Starving with the poor.

He calls himself a prince.
I thought the race was dead.
His genealogy has, since
A century, been said
To carry in its veins
Clear traces of the mad.

Prince Madness, tell me, when you speak
Through foam upon your lips,
Are you the frontispiece of God,
Or just a human lapse?

I beg you, take this fool away,
And bury him afar.
I am well enough to face the day
Without another prayer.

Courage

He refused to accept defeat.
Unless there were some overwhelming
Reason. Such as death.

Rather a flurry of propositions,
Tall tales of love
In a dusty alley off the avenue.

The smell of a sweet rose
In winter. A realistic ballad
With an improbable ending.

What proposal for heroics?
Curs snarl only
At the feet of cowards.

The snatched moment of joy
In the anonymous suburb
Marks up another victory.

The secret is to choose the ultimate
Proposition. With the right
Words of benediction.

Not a Serious Defect

"Certain persons told him that he was mad; but
that was not looked upon as a serious defect."
- The House of the Dead.

He walked an unfamiliar path
Unbecoming round
Trailing his own reality
The limits of the town

And taking April by
Married his wits to Spring
No harm to match them to
The melody he sang

The time he went was bound
By winter but today
Is April and the bonds
Are carelessly laid down

Then carefully put away
Folded with the weight
Of solitudes too long
In the cupboards of the night

Anxiously he walked mad
Through the exacting bornes
Searching new words ready-made
To meld into his song

Where no two souls grate
One upon the other
And in the hugely quiet sky
Two stilled birds hover

Magic in the cloudless air
To fight the sickness in the bone
But no-one else to travel there
No-one a hand to offer.

The Friend of the Family

Although there, friendly, obsequious, ready
To extend a seemingly helping hand,

Why do I hesitate to grasp it when
I need an advocate?

Suspicion grows in the night,
Or perhaps I want alone to be

My only defender,
Thus rejecting for all the family

The chance of even
A half-hearted support,

Or a foolish word,
Of ineffective encouragement.

Anyway I am certain if ever
I were desperate in the maze

Of night I would find no trace
Of him. So I must go separately

On my way and forget
His smiling day-time face.

The Double

Poor people wandering like a task
Force of love are not all alone.
They have their doppel-ganger, double,
Sosie, dvoinik not far away.

Just out of reach, beyond the mirror,
The ghost of a man, a laugh
In the dark streets, drifting like a wraith
Through the back-alleys of the mind.

And no-one can be sure, like Councillor
Golyadkin, that he will not be
Escorted that very night from life's
Bureaucracy into the arms
Of the lunatic asylum.

Ernst Neizvestny, Illustration for Dostoyevsky's novel "Crime and Punishment".

The Egoism of Suffering

Walking down the Moika
One early evening a few years ago,
In time and place so little
Changed from his St. Petersburg,
Suddenly, almost seeing
As if carved from the leaden sky,
Giving so small a space for mortals
Between the burdensome clouds
And the flat, gray land, suddenly
Those frightening words...She
Plunged with pleasure into pain
And that egoism of suffering...

This was only Natasha.
But I saw there somehow
All Russia..."one must suffer
To the end for future happiness."
And who else could know?
These people in their shabby clothes,
Hugging their terrible memories,
Walking almost mindlessly
Past the great palaces
And the tormented slums,
Indifferent to each.
Plunged only into their own
Secretly guarded souls.

Petersburg Days

The pasty sky hangs over the city
Like an assasin's hand, the sun,
Just above the line of December,
Waiting out the few hours of its time.

We wait too, wondering, fearful
Of the long northern night, numbering
The days before the solstice turns.
The sky becomes suddenly lighter, though
The sun is hidden now.

Snow begins to fall from the porous
Clouds, small crystalline flakes
That throw a curtain of luminosity
Across us, obscuring the condemned
Who in dark alleys also wait.

They are our brothers. They differ only
Because they do not need to count the days.
It has been done for them.

The Humiliated......

The humiliated are inevitably oppressed
And the oppressed humiliated.
The strong are strong by night
And frightening by day.
Why bother with those
Who cannot fight?
Or trouble with them
Who are the simple prey
Of the bigger, the better and the best?

The universe winds down.
All worlds dissolve. "Suffering
Purifies all...." The offended
Think it is the way to
Future happiness; and buy it
At the price of torment.

Since my distant enemy
Is hardly known and his shape
Unclear, I prefer a short
Untroubled space with you
In the certain knowledge
That all matter decomposes,
With these words, leaving only
The obscure power of vegetation.

Anarchists

> "..............Revolution
> Is the affair of logical lunatics."
> - Wallace Stevens ("L'Esthetique du Mal")

They take their dreams to the market
Place but end up stuffed in the garbage
Heap of history. Their words
Are bloated with the impossible.

They are propelled by some
Internal combustion that ignores
The laws of science.

They are constipated by logic
And turned inside out by hate.

They have an answer for the absolute
But they are likely to drown
In the foul water of the gutter
Because they are unaware
Sewers even exist.
And are fatal for lunatics.

His

A Message from Beyond

The winter is sick.
All the troubled dead
In their frozen cemeteries
Are ready, more ready
Than in the compassion
Of summer, to break
Their chains and join
The ghouls in the mortuary.

He puts his hand in yours
With a message for you, alone:
That sound was not the dead
But the sound of feet
Advancing little by little
Over the brittle ground.
And the message said
It is not a fatal malady.

There is a cure, there are
Prescriptions against the plague.

Bobok

Scratched at the door of death,
Knowing the aperture was there
From the smell, the stench
Of the soul.

Locked up
In the psychiatric ward,
To make sure we are all sane.

Tied neatly in a shroud.
Silenced in the shadow of night.

To be sensible a man
Must call himself a fool
Once in a while.

To be part
Of God means to sell
His spirit to the third
Level of humankind.

And wash his feet and hands
In atomic dust.

Innocent Snow

It was twenty below again last night.
I can see only dimly through the frosted
Glaze of my window. The sun sparkles
On the snow already beginning in places
Where man passed to turn to dirty gray.
But elsewhere beyond the fence in the open
Field it is still a dazzling white.

A tree bent and almost broken by
A previous ice storm, which has left
Its fine but probably fatal decoration
On it and the cedar hedge, stands token
To savagery. Under the stunning blue
Of the cloudless sky not a bird flies.
Those that had the courage to stay
With us this long time are either
Sheltering where they may, though I
Cannot fathom where, or hang frozen
To the trees ice sculpture.

Although obsessed by the deadly beauty
Before me I feel resentment.
I do not rage at God but burn within
Like the possessed, and remember Siberia.
The landscape is the same but I know there
Under the virgin snow lie the unjust dead.

I look again at the cold expanse
And the innocent snow. Our nature
Now seems less unfair. The challenge
I accept, the rest forgive.

Terrorists

> "Je meprise cette poussiere qui me
> compose et qui vous parle."
>
> - Saint-Just

Living outside one's self
Ignoring the web of the universe
And the quickly rotting fabric
Of the body it is easy
To transmit this liberation
Of the spirit to those about to die
In the supreme egotism
Governing the invented
Actor on a supposed stage
Existing only in their vision
of history

Underground

> "I confess in all humility that I am at quite a
> loss to understand why it has all to be so."
> — Ivan Karamazov

In a small crevice of the soul
There is a fury that even
In our ordinary times must be
Nourished with care every
Hour, every day. Old age
Needs it more. Fire: not
To forget nor blur the edge
Of before.

       Particulary
Underground: The soot-grimed
Miner in every-one trying
With muted desperation
To break out of the lode
That runs in us.
Or maybe the weight of some
Undetermined guilt.
The heritage of Christendom.

Shock it all off if you can,
And look clear-eyed
At the tentacles of dawn
Justt gropiing beyond
The ice-cold lake waters
And the green-black hills.
What lies underground is
Of no import. Provided
You let the prisoner out.

III - *The Window*

Solitude

Listening beside my half-open window,
Which I ought to close, so my doctor tells me,
To avoid further complications in my lungs,
Not to mention arthritis and various other
Hinted at malfunctions of an aging body,
I hear first sounds of Spring, an illusive
Whisper which I cannot easily identify.

It lifts up from the river-bed through
The early morning ground fog which in a few
Minutes will slip away leaving the tree
Trunks black still against patches of dirty snow,

A young man, I cannot see him well,
Comes into view carrying a newspaper
In one hand and something fixed to his head.
Unaware of the Spring he is listening to the most
Recent rock and he skips in time. No he is not
Entirely unaware. He is humming and a happy
Smile washes his face. To my greeting
He lifts a hand, but he is already out
Of my sphere. Unlike an early robin
Which I can justifiably claim part of.

I push back my chair not wanting
To close out the Spring but feeling in my bones
The treachery of the air. It is easy
To have pure thoughts and a blameless life
If you are condemned to solitude.

"They who have no arms
Have cleanest hands," Dylan said that
It seems so long ago. Pure song,
Pure spirit in a chastened cell.

The solitude is better in the morning light.
Even at dawn, with some promise

Of the better, it is a burden, and lying awake
Alone is a fruitless thing.

But that first Spring day pays well
For all the haunting past.

467

Ernst Neizvestny, Illustrations for Dostoyevsky's novel "Crime and Punishment".

The Sound of Tears

I am saddened by the sound of rusted
Leaves in the ditch of autumn,
Rusted cars in the scrap-heap
Of the distant suburb,
Of weeds growing in scratched fields,
Of chalk in the winter pits,

The sound of paint peeling
On slum doors,
Of misery in a child's
Lost and forlorn eyes,

The sound of snow in a
New and windless night,
Of wood waiting by the hearth,
Of a smile which does not come,
In a winter which has made me deaf.

Above all the sound of tears
Between two chasms of sleep.

Naming a Flower

My neighbour, supposedly mad,
Has laid a flower on my window-sill
Suddenly verdant with Spring.
With his curious and encylopedic
Mind he begins to name its parts.

This is the corolla, he says, and then
The stigma, the style, the anther,
Stamen, ovary, torus, sepal,
Calyx, ovula...and I stare appalled.

This little bloom was a few
Minutes before so beautiful.
Now as his pedantic finger points
At all those identified parts,
Each no doubt with its defined
Function, the flower fades
Into a piece of high technology.

And I remember my sergeant
Defining the parts of a gun,
Each with its specific aim
All adding up to a lethal whole.

No naming of parts, though, can
Destroy the glory in my odd
Friend's face, as he displays
His knowledge, nor efface
The air of mystery in the April bud.

Before the Gate

"Todo lo vivo que pasa
Por las puertas de la muerte
Va con la cabeza baja
Y un aire blanco durmiente"
    —Federico Garcia Lorca ("Cigarra")

If I should lose myself
One morning suddenly
A morning without you
A morning of sick with loneliness
Let me look elsewhere
Than the gate bloodied
With dawn.

        And let me
Hold up my head so you
May see my eyes are not
Closed or afraid of my face
Pale. After all
I have been half way
Through many times before
And have turned back
Providentially.

But I am a sleep-
Walker in white nights
That spread like snow
Across an unfamiliar
Landscape. And it is easy
To take another path

Ending before that gate
Which speaks as stones
Speak in words that
Need not be translated.

The Eccentric

My neighbour taps on my window,
It is too cold to open but I can
Understand from long conversations
Of the deaf.

       His fingers
In the winter night have
Overflowed and spread into
The village streets. He does not
Need my help, just my sympathy
To keep him company until
They can be collected and
Brought back.

       Generally
He is considered mad but not
Yet certifiable. Perhaps in a more
Perfect city he would be already
In the psychiatric ward.
But the villagers are tolerant
And smile.

       As I do.
Grateful for a touch
Of the improbable, and happy
To share an important secret
With an unimportant soul.

Near Dawn

Unable to sleep I become
Part of every sound in the night.

I gather them all into my being
In a sensual osmosis.

Hoping they will form
A pattern to forgetfulness.

But the noises become
Only a staccato farce.

And the dawn seems far
And a very improbable ending.

After the Rain

The stains on the wall
Spread like the plague

It is not raining now
But the air is heavy

And the clouds seem
Almost one with the earth

Under the sodden
Leaves stealthily

Rises a tenuous
Sliver of smoke

Boundless always
As an afterthought

The smell recalling
Fire in the cellar

And there is no change
In the habitual silence

That clasps solidly
My small acre

The Real Dimension

> "I have hardly anything in common
> with myself and should stand very quietly in
> a corner, content that I can breathe."
> Franz Kafka — diary

My window becomes a mirror
And increasingly I fear to look
Through it, anticipating less
The outside world than
The incompetent copy of myself
I am bound to see there.

       Incompetent
And certainly drawn with false
Perspective, but faithful.
Whether better or worse who
Knows. At times just barely
Recognizable. Still not entirely
Detestable, so my neighbour thinks.

But I doubt his judgement.
He thinks the world is flat.

It is hard to find the real
Dimension. I look deep
Into myself and scan the past,
Or what I know of it. It resembles
Very little that image through
The dusty pane of glass.

I would prefer to go back
Into a niche of time and sit
Absolutely still, shaping quietly
A dimension which fits
And with which I can exist.

61

A Child at Midnight

He looks through his fingers
In the endless December night
Held up to the shade his face
Against a non-existent sun.

Still the sky is clear and some
Light filters into the room.
He does not try to block it out,
But absorb it into those small
Objects which in the dark
Attach themselves to him.

At noon they have no significance,
The familiar having nothing
To alarm. But at midnight
They seem shrill with menace,
Undefined but real.

        The moon
Suddenly appears, reducing
To rubbish any thought
Of anguish. But there are hours
Yet to go, and so many shadows
On the road to dawn.

Contemporary Thinking

Now my window is slightly glazed —
The temperature dropped during the night —
But through the tracery of the frost
I can see the world well enough.

A dog, a cur without doubt, blind,
No, blind in one eye only, a gaping
Hole the colour of chalk or putty,
Ambles across the snow that fell
Without notice through my sleep,
Leaving a pattern inconsistent
With his rough look.

       He pauses,
Sees me behind the pane, puzzled,
Then with a kind of shrug moves
To the cypress hedge and cautiously
Lifts a clumsy leg to stain
The snow. Like the wild dogs
On the white sand of Sinai,
Or around the Catacombs.

I am tempted by War Games
On my video, but today have no
Appetite for something so
Like the real thing. Chess with
My computer perhaps, but he
Always wins, whoever he is.
I look in the book of instructions.
Bobby Fischer programmed that
Disturbing foe I have come to hate.

      So I turn back to
Dryden a bit, and Henry James —
"The Princess Casamassima."
His terrorists are innocent
Amateurs. A Hassan Abri has just

Claimed credit for killing forty-one
People in a Paris shopping-mall.
So I turn off the news. It's not
Exactly new.

   I am safe, they say.
Unless there is defective wiring
And my house blows up. So you
Close your eyes, cover your
Ears, wipe out memory. You were
Never part of it, never responsible.
No unjust treaty signed through
Negligence. You were a witness
Only, and those who stand
Aside cannot be guilty. That
Is the practice, and the law.
I think........

The dog, the cur, comes shuffling back.
He has a torn packet in his ugly
Mouth. Again he stops, resolutely
This time, before my diminishing
Window, projecting his one eye like
A spot-light, then deliberately
Shakes out, so I can see, a half
Obliterated map of things gone wrong.

He is solid as a stone, and alone
As a shadow of history.
It is very cold, his breath
Is mist, his feet attached to
The snow, nailed to the ground
Below. I force the window open
And shout, but he will not go.
He stands firm like melancholy.
Even his vacant eye of chalk
Has some portion of reproach.

Shutting the window, pulling down
The blind is no help. He is still
There, a gray silhouette tied
To the past. I try to think
Positively, to call the police.
But they cannot chase ghosts
Or put behind bars memories.

So I trust when the time is ripe
He will go on about his business
And possible I can once more
Look out unruffled on that
Almost untouched snow.

Reading in the Dark

In the night I can see
But by day my eyes
Squint vaguely into the sun

Strangely I can read
The philosophers at midnight
But scarcely scan

Your name at noon
In the dark I conjure up
New adjectives for you

And they seem as fresh
As Spenser as quaint
As Blake although at dawn

I cannot remember them
Nor can I see your face
Or the books I try to read

Early October Insomnia

Outside the rain
Slowly turning to snow

Great gray slow
Flakes that pause

As they pass
My window

Distorted in the glass
Twisting like paste

Dancers in stopped
Rhythm when

The pane cracks
Something comes apart

The air is cold
I shiver to the bone

I can't remember
Was October ever

January things
Disintegrating

Stars invisible
Drifting apart

The months to come
Unreal disordered

The rain should be
Water still

Not these crude
Unseasonable

Self-destructing
Winter pieces

Here take hold
My hand so

Something like a wall
To lean against

Steady solid
In the unlikely

Premature
Freezing wind

Tell me that your
Mind is strong

Your body warm
Your calendar

Right the season
Wrong the storm

Gone the rain
Sweet winter not

With us yet our
Time stretched out

Enough to bear
In the still dark dawn

Another hour here

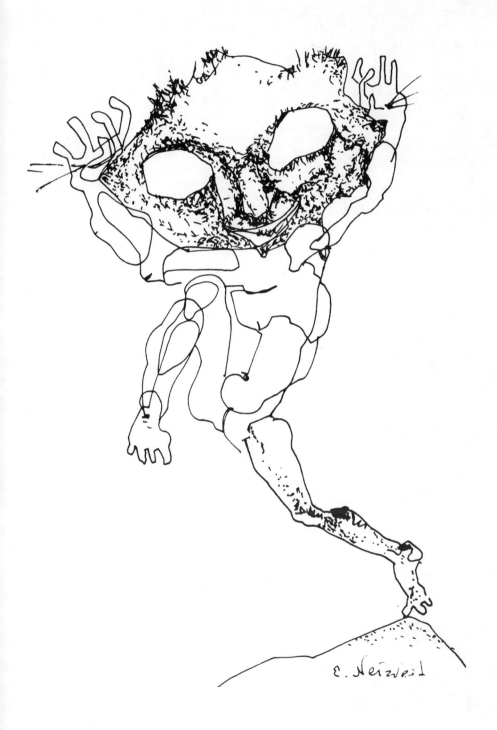

Ernst Neizvestny, Etching from the "Fate" Series.

February Midnight

Burdened with insomnia
The windows in the tight houses
Of the cheap suburb
Throw faint light
On the February snow
Of a winter lengthening
Into months that should
Soon in principle be Spring

But they seem fixed
In false astronomy
And sleeplessness
Wears out the will to resist.

IV - *The Wound and the Bow*

Unexplored Geography

I have wasted too much time
Searching for an unmapped
Corner of the mind
Where I can lie down quietly
And draw dreams of fleeting clouds
And rain on upturned faces.

And devise a philosophy,
Socio-political, of course,
That will encompass the poles
And track the uncatalogued
Crevices and glaciers
That haunt me night and day.

All the unexplored remnants
Of geography left us still
By the technicians of our age
If any yet exist some virgin
Land some nameless mount
Some prairie beckoning
To infinity.

The Wound and the Bow

    - Philoctetes

There was a time
I see it now
The narrow streets
Were banked with snow

The milk vans ran
On wooden sleds
The horses slipping
With their loads

God gave me memory
Those days are here
And not forgotten
With the years

All the important
Things between
War revolutions
Some presidents a queen

Are blurred like the haze
On that distant day
When at twenty below
A crippled boy

First fell on the ice
And struggled there
Implored his god
And made a prayer

To caulk the wound
And bind the limb
And shoot his arrow
Against the wind

74

Lake Huron

We who grew up in the alleged
Centre of the continent
Thought the blue waters of Huron
The sea. And the grey breakers
When the west wind blew
As big as houses on any
Far Atlantic shore.

Mysterious for me it harboured
Moby Dick and the Old Man.
The legends of the Hurons
And the Iroquois more real
Than Ulysses. The War
Canoes greater the any
Trireme of an improbable past.

The sun in winter seemed
To wait on the faint line
Of a so distant horizon
To be summoned home
Into a west that had no
Further land. Michigan
Was there somewhere but
It was an unlikely place
As far away as Columbia.

And when I look now
From the cliffs of Goderich
I feel still a small relic
Of that childhood mystery,
A tremor of awe at that azure
Ocean that somehow
Should not be there.

The Hill Farm

In the rough stones of the wall
Encircling the hill-side orchard,
One small flower whose name
I know not blooms in the crevices,
Bursting with joy, as in the improbable
Corners of the heart.

Autumn in the Bourbonnais

I am almost in the geographical
Centre of France. I spread out
My arms to the far corners
Of the Hexagon and breathe in
The evasive odours and timid
Contours of this subtle land.

In the hills there is a vivid
Splash of colour, a red
Like the maples of my own
Far Gatineau. But no rough
Slope drenched in scarlet.

No golden shower across
The horizon and under-foot,
Lasting so briefly in its
Challenge to winter. Melancholy
Rather in the slow changing
Of leaves to brown and yellow.

The cut wood is stacked
In perfect lines as if
Waiting for a customer,
Homogenised, without
Odour, no strong smell of pine.

But in a cottage yard
Leaves are burning in a neat
Heap. And the smoke is the same
As it was along the Ottawa.
And it hurts me in the heart.

A Child in the Woods

Here is reality instead. Which is not
Recoverable in the disintegrating
Body. A word or two based
On the candour of a child's tongue.
Words like the scent of wisteria
On a Spring day and as short-lived.
Sounds intangible, but yet
More real than hard bone and horn.

Death in the woods is something
Our everyday violence has not
Prepared him for. It's not real.
It is a myth the October leaves
Artfully conceal.

       He turns away
And, catching sight of a Death's Head
Moth, transforms delight
Into the wonder of speech.

A Child Dying

In the tropic night
A child's cry becomes
An explosion of anguish.

Awakened suddenly, not
By the child in the dark,
But the negative,

Stifling perfume
Of the unreal flowers,
I fight insomnia, yet,

Identifying with the cry,
Now a whimper that
Gradually runs down.

As my will turns to stasis,
As my world seems to wither
In the endless night.

And when the sun comes
Abruptly, I wonder
If it will give me

Back the energy to flee
My shadow. Standing
With eyes wide open,

I take in yet the glory
Of the blooms which
In the night had seemed

Only a sickening odour
Accompanying a child
In his early and last agony.

Silence

Silence comes back again,
And frequently after.
Something you can see,
Taking the form of heavy seas
Not breaking, or even
The movement of a bee,
Wings almost invisible,
Not buzzing in the mid-day air.

When the feel
Of silence becomes intolerable
I destroy the image
And consume what remains.

All that is left is a word
That can be touched,
An absence that is real,
A silence that can be heard.

Distances

Before and beyond this pale child
With a face the colour of chalk
The marshalling yards throw out a web
Of inconsistencies which we, who know,
Know conceal by their deceptions
Some rails that lead some place.

A logic of sorts hides there somehow.
And a ticking brain exists behind the stark
Naked eyes and the frail frame.
Although it cannot contemplate
Rationally a long journey into the unknown,
That brain takes stock.

And eventually decides which lines
Run where and why and to what far port.
With a magic name. Not to go anywhere
Makes him shrink even more
And close his thin arms around a dream.
Anyway the yards are shut. There are no trains.

To my sorrow that port I know.
The syllables of its name evoke
Mystery but it stinks of garbage
In the sun and bodies in its slums.
When I try to penetrate those eyes my talk
Turns to nothing. And sadly I look
Away from that exhausted face
And those fragile limbs.

Tropic Night

In the tropic night my words
Are lost in the limpid waters
Of a dream. You are there
Without sound but I know
You are listening.

The sheets are clammy though
The rain stopped a dream ago.
The silence alters one degree
As a humid air suddenly
Stirs the jacaranda and its
Leaves scrape against each other.

In staged geometry drawn
Back, the covers on our bed of love
Design an after-thought,
And take the conversation of the night
Into the calculus of dawn.

quiet

Misinterpretation

On the cluttered balconies of the poor
There is no shield against the sun.
The air moves intermittently,
Almost as hot as in the alleys
And the blistering streets.

Yet I hear no word of complaint.
On the contrary what seemed
To my untuned ear a faint
Whisper of love. But perhaps the noise
Of the tropics translated
Badly the sound of an old man
Dying in the night.

A Tropical Fish

I ask you in the net to see
The foliation of a coral bed
And a fish in poisonous colour
Desperate in its struggle

Take the wrong way to death
Wasting all its valour
Plunging toward the depths
In its hopeless battle

Poison served so little
Courage even less
The colours become coral
The black water red

Ernst Neizvestny, Etching from "Crime and Punishment".

Antennae

Is this a season
When hands become eyes
Leading us half-blind
Out of the hatred of winter?

We extend them like antennae
Before us. They must act
For all our organs.

Waiting for the touch,
The feel of Spring,
The smell of a breeze,
The sound of happiness.

Speaking with hands and eyes,
And putting underground
The last whimper of winter.

The School of Fear

I should enroll
In some learned school
That teaches at least
The rudiments of fear.

I need it to survive
In this ancient place.
If you know fear
You know the worst.

And if you find less
Than truth the waste
Destroys and the best
Path is lost.

Why

I have turned my thoughts
To where and everything to why not
That I cannot fully recall
How winter goes or fall
Days turn summer sour
And the philosophers dry
Up or all all always
Your smile remains your
Questioning look as if still
Asking why and awaiting
An answer somewhere

Gaza

Look
   at the little words
      sliding off
         this page

Like
   the sands of Gaza
      every pebble
         moving

Imperceptibly
   before the desert wind
      towards its
         inevitable

Destination
   apparently into
      the sea more
         probably

Towards
  Jerusalem
    I wish they could be
      converted

On their way
   and become
      true words
         of reconciliation

For an Israeli Poet

I never met Moshe Dor.
In fact I've never been to Jerusalem.
Looked meditatively once years ago
Across the Blue Line from the squalid
Fields of Gaza
Unto the green banks of Israel.

This must have been about the time
He began writing, in war, and then
War again and again. But love
Was never lost in the haze of the desert
Churned up by tanks and the ephemeral
Ghost of victory. And "strange birds flying"
In the vault of heaven.

It is a small miracle then
To write of love, and Xanadu. but maybe
The miracle is in the land. And we,
Standing continents, and centuries apart,
Can only speculate on real heroics.
And wonder they can breed poets.

Cryptogram in the Rain

There is a smear of rain
On the gray plaster wall,
And dark rivulets extend
Slowly down the grain,
Drawing pure sentiment
Into documents extant,
Sweating in the summer air.

Documents invented as the mind
With an unsure touch reveals
In that subtle new design
Some harmony with the wish
To create and recreate a life-time,
Hopefully well spent,
Approaching its happy end.

Invention in the haphazard
Test of rain-drops on a wall
Supports the active brain,
Prolongs the twilight zone,
And gives an hour more
To analyse the past,
Project some happy dawn.

Getting the Message Straight

I am searching for the right verb
To tell you that I am coming after all

But I do not want an impious word
Or a message distorted

It is almost as important
As the coming itself to put it right

It is not logical but still
When I arrive and you have heard

And you have read the signal
You must know that love

Has justified the journey

V - *The Shortest Poem*

The Moon Is Finished

Almost all Russians were fascinated by the first land-
ing on the moon on July 20, 1969. Some, the political figures
above all, were annoyed at the American technical success
which caught the imagination of the whole world and by one
act restored American prestige and destroyed the Soviet lead
in space research and exploration. The military were dis-
turbed by its strategic implications. The scientists were
unhappy at the American break-through but at the same
time deeply interested by this advance in space travel. The
average Russian was simply intrigued as were most people
in the world by the extraordinary idea of a human being, no
matter what his nationality, actually walking on the surface
of the moon.

But the most original reaction came from my friend,
the poet Andrei Voznesensky. A few weeks after Neil
Armstrong's adventure I had tea with Andrei at his dacha in
Peredelkino, not far from the former home of Boris Paster-
nak. Inevitably the subject of moon travel came up. Andrei
said he had been both depressed and elated by the achieve-
ment. He had even written a poem about it. He rose, fetched
a piece of paper and wrote, or rather designed the following:

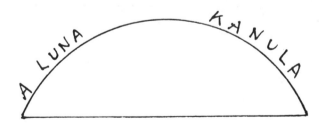

"That is my reaction to the man on the moon", he said.

Literally it means "The moon has vanished", and is written so that it can be read from left to right and right to left. At the same time the arc as a visual poem represented the moon in decline. But, Andrei explained, he really meant that the moon was "finished". Not in the literal sense but in the imagination and fantasy of mankind. He concluded that the role that mysterious orb has played in literature, and above all in poetry, was gone forever. No longer could any-one think of the moon in the old way. It was now proved to be a substantial, solid piece of soil, no different in texture from the Gobi or the Mojave Desert.

So, in his puckish way, Andrei wrote his shortest poem, perhaps the world's shortest, making even Haiku appear long-winded. And yet the poem packs, syllable for syllable, a vast amount of meaning. And, alas, without that clever combination of sounds, rhyme and letters, untranslateable into an English poem.

I recall vividly that afternoon in a strictly Checkovian setting, the nineteenth century cottage, ancient wicker furniture, the inevitable samovar, tea and honey, the grass in the garden, as always over-grown. A scene as remote from our own society as one could imagine and yet comfortable and adequate in its own way. A young poet looking with nostalgia at the sky and drawing the arc of the vanished moon in verse on a scrap of paper.

VI - *Pozzi*

Ernst Neizvestny, "Cyclops". Drawing, Indian ink and colour. 1977.

Catherine Pozzi, 1882-1934, was a unique product of the Parisian world of arts and letters which flourished with extraordinary brilliance during her lifetime. She was a friend and correspondent of almost every well-known writer or thinker of that epoch. Her book "Peau d'Ame" expressed her philosophic system which combined gnosticism and Indian wisdom with modern concepts of biology and physics, in particular with regard to heredity and entropy.

A grave illness drastically reduced her activities after 1917 and her poetic output was small. But the delicacy of her verse, in a form almost like filigree, cannot obscure the intensity of the emotions they express.

Andre Gide included her poems in his classic *"Anthology of French Poetry"*. The American scholar Lawrence Joseph is now working on a definitive biography. The five poems I have translated are, to the best of my knowledge, the first version in English of her poetry and have been approved by her son, the French writer and Resistance Fighter, Claude Bourdet.

Nova

In a world beyond time where I will have
A life not formed in the sky of everyday,
In that new space where my will is swept away,
In that new-born star from which I flee,
You will live, my splendour, my misfortune, my survival,
My most very heart made of the blood I am,
My breath, my touch, my glance, my envious desire,
My most worldly boon lost to infinity.

Maya

I descend the steps of centuries and sand
Handing back to you this very time and its despair
Land of golden temples, I enter into your fable
          Adored Atlantica

From a body which is nothing more to me
          which flees at last the flames
The soul is a dear name hated by destiny —
Let time stop, let the weft unravel,
I retrace my steps towards the abyss of childhood.

The birds on the western seawind are in flight,
One must fly, happiness, to the mythic summer
Profoundly asleep where the shore ends

Rocks, song, king, tree so long cradled
Stars so long a time attached to my first face

Singular sun crowned with calm

Scopolamine

The wine which flows in my veins
Has drowned my heart and won the day
And I will navigate the sky
On board a heart without a captain
Where oblivion like honey melts away.

My heart is like a new-found star
Which floats, divine, unparalleled.
Adrift, grown strange!
O voyage towards sun
A new and constant sound
Becomes the fabric of your sleep.

My heart has fled my story
Farewell Form I feel no more
I am saved I am lost
I search in the far unknown
A name free of memory.

Nyx

O you my night, O awaited darkness
O proud country, O stubborn secrets
O long regards, O crushing nakedness
O flight permitted beyond closed skies,

O great desire, O vast surprise
O lovely course of spirit charmed
O worst of evils, O fallen grace,
O open door where none has passed,

I know not why I die and drown
Before entering the eternal abode,
I do not know whose prey I am.

Ave

My very great love, if I should die
Without knowing how I you possessed
In what sun you dwelled,
In what past your time, in what hour
    Was my love for you,

My very great love, beyond memory,
Fire without hearth of which I made my day,
In what fate you traced my history,
In what sleep was your glory seen,
    O my sojourn

When I shall be lost for myself
And divided in the infinite abyss,
Infinitely, when I shall be shattered,
When the present in which I am clothed
    Will have betrayed,

By a universe in a thousand bodies broken
Of a thousand instants unassembled,
Of ashes winnowed in the empty skies,
You will remake for a strange year
    One treasure only,

You will remake my name and my image,
Of thousand pieces blown away,
Living unity without name or visage,
Heart of the spirit, O centre of the mirage,
    My very great love.